X

5/00

TIM DAVIS

DAILIES

THE FIGURES

— m — 3/00 $ 13.00

Cover and interior design by the focus group of Dirk Rowntree,
Elizabeth Elsas & Viola C. Garr.

Some of these poems have appeared in the following publications:
*Aerial, Apex of the M, Boo, Crayon, First Intensity, FiveFingers Review,
Lingo, Murmur, Object, Passages, Poetry Project Newsletter, Shiny,
Snare,Torque,* & *The Washington Review.*

Frontispiece photo by Seth Rubin: "Impression of a Book in Flour," 1998

THE FIGURES, 5 Castle Hill, Great Barrington, MA, 01230
Distributed by Small Press Distribution, 1341 Seventh Avenue,
Berkeley, CA 97710-1403, www.spd.org

The publisher wishes to thank Hand Hollow Foundation, the Saul
Rosen Foundation, and the ever mysterious Fund for Poetry for gen-
erous support.

For the law firm of
Stefans, Fitterman, Davies & Smith

also the infield of Fagin to
Gizzi to Young

and for Mom

and Empleomania

| CONTENTS |

DAILIES

Dailies was written by some certain 9-5-lifer waking up one lunch hour and noticing he wasn't sure he was the same poet who had started yesterday's bright little title fight. A "force quit" command was installed on the keyboard, dumping every day's piecework into midnight pumpkindom. The method was investigative and shattered: compose, audit, toggle all you want—during coffee breaks, morning blear, elevator going up—and after bedtime punch the clock. Then with two years service, a full-scale review of what sort of poet-worker we were here. Note that the movement from "one day's nose in the ass of the next" [*12/31*] to "just another budgeted triumphant brother" [*12/31*] might not represent promotion. Many of the poems are rushed and crabby—even this key to the executive washroom was faxed off hastily on my very last day. The book runs backwards because—we can only hope.

let us raise our caste and ask it
how the showmen itemize the mighty

let us toast foist
that a libidinous inbred ibid (in
crippled billfold)
might coin another active owe

as the hezbollah have owed the shorebirds borscht
as our prodigies have cornered markets on faux capital so-so
you hear the 3-D eagle ogling?

in bettered times
a menthol enmity
might send home flaubert's flatworm
without christian-millennium fingered-over din din

but where was i, bad hair life
while the holepunchers fell on the month of enough
while this "chum consanguine evening"
foaled befuddled bloodletters into mister better world

here's to who fears *here's to*
since your tears aren't shed but sweated
the guy in the mining company who, um, names the claims
just another budgeted triumphant brother
pinch me when the attribution ends

friends, odds are
evening by the side you're on
would that we might dozer closer to the median
the commonplace book of done gone over this is

gurgitated into UN bluecaps
the shiftscape has landed
rifling, reaping, and reseeding (there were three more r's)
there were too falutin right-to-25-to-lifers to resist

i propose a broach
you've a oom-pah uvula, go ahead and
gulp up journalissimus
until it billows silhouettes of killer zeroes

with this ich bin
rid of this

everything is tiered
and ignorant of it

let there be merrymarking
another round of gummy worms and frank placebos squirreled
distributed is what *lang syne* will mean
west of where the camera unzips your pants

the low quotidian bode

haze between the moon and me
spielberg (meaning storyland) on gilbert and sullivan:
"the very model"
say *dollar* in that way
praise ramadan in forest hills for shag red flags
it poetcheapens constant spree

if something nice, say,
you can fangle breughel throw rugs
the hybrid roslyn carters haven't held on through the frost
d (for down quark) day long faded
half high to stoplight herpes
there be 'some nerve' how it's worded

plant a fatty on the filtered veil
you've waved to global chafing
the supplier to the barrow to the kiosk of the creeds
in perpetuam ignoramus, paris
in the former, ulan bator in the next
meantime check in case the kids are slaking

admission at crossed grift

her foot up
on a greyhound bubble

mug the margin, wipers, driver's seat
burst a blear drum listening, truss a duct

how am i to ham-eye movement?
her full femurness or
converse in extremis?

hawk eye back in head with good book
visual world means rubber baby, everybody formerly!

dr. acquiesce no more notices
the back of the bus untangling than it's
foot fetishists keeping fahrenheit alive

i was wither, mister lint
processed cheese does not pre-teen the essay form
in fact there's no way to de-mean
(apart from jacking out the gas)

let's see guillotined cerebrum
remember fashion-conscious ass

what a poached giraffe'd ponder

love a loath newtonian fruit compote

there will always be another
thruwayan foot in the foreground going

wars over voiceovers

i fought the law and
you can turn the world on with your smile

the lives spent
desperately circumcising santa
(whose goose is raw)
whose public act is loosed

the sound of one holiday tin of deviled bumblebee decaying

less than celebrittle
persons half a stork and half a rubber raft
bend to miff their laces

jealousy and crummy dubbing
judgment come what
primordial macaroon
rain down on 'getting gruntled'

feedbirds' bleeping rebirth
(cog in lockstep) awholemouthfulof'em

o little slur of bethlehaw

milli vanilli on content
drawn agog in the epiglottis thaw

identify with the characters' can't
happen then: i'll have huffed

lots of love,
future perfect mouthings of the picture perfect house down

lonely ethnic droll

no fly zone essence estimate
let the buyer bet the liar
...but they weren't developed

developed estimata
cran-actionable branded pillow pageant
if a supermodel'd written this
if the secretary general

lily lactose guerrilla
skated back from jiminy
mini-mart with the redi-whip

and cunningly numbingly above
pyong yang has sent a manned mission
the elopement of marcuse
and a telemarketer from land's end

and send deenforcements
why wait when the death toll can
stay distorted

it is aid
in the form of flame

dear liary:

what the davening go-bots wrote,
in soap, of their own hairs,
an isthmus list pronating toward entirety
a shopper's guide to civil war thimbles
the score of showboat imagined for a cast of cans

and what the public-private partnership kept
cuddled in its border,
a biography of botha called salacious in the trades
another outdated primer on viability
linking melancholy CIA agents to e.m. cioran

with what full dealt frontal
besides an infinite number of archaeological finds
timed so the whole world's swallowed molly bolts
lining letter jackets with irration cards
and vertigo repair kits with the family circle seal

why the media is the lymph of myths
a parboiled load-bearing header
parsed *forceps, marijuana, paint fumes, korsakoff's*
all ways to hunt lame ducks on tame ponds
with your hands a different market than your hunger

anti-daylight-savings-time-anthem

with Vic Chesnutt

in a land where the neighbors have
a refrigerator full of rats
the children learn the cello and are tender

if the defrostation time of
chicken pie is not adhered to

if the babysitter willly
points to where *they* buried *them*

gone finally the rescued greyhound's lacerations
and the nightly news while exercycling castaway toyota keys

o, home, o
prone to champing at the chewables
wind up on the skim milk carton, halftone and turning bad

when conditions mean a slicker and no discman
up at six to finish chinua achebe book report
and from the lab at school
extra credit deglitching the computer on the combine

spoils agribusiness timecards

lord, won't you please help me get a loan

let's call the pall 'practicable'

to harvest crispy hexagons again
earning a degree in it

hey creatúre

skin, bone, or foe
as if dose of pencil in
a moon of immunities
is to mention
and then a billboard mention

mid to
tabled 70s reprise sinatra
audible only underwater
at the fontainbleu hotel

every ginkgo has a guardrail

border double, who'll play park chung hee?

this one's called unteetered

paints lashes on their mergers and acquisitions fuck doll

candide camera, kasha varnishkes

in california
a sand in the marketshare abrasive morning DJ
assails emissions testing noah's ark

build a mintier breathalyzer
like a virgin, live to tell
a jury of your exes, *carpe* AARP larder

would that customs confiscated storyboards
the christmases that talked up physiognomy

leeks in the garden tendril depth charge neighbor's cable

the crazier...my inner bailiff
passed the barre stones, say "waste treatment"
velvet curtain between un and non
between half- and left-wit
the pastime will be straddle and concur

12 steps in 3 acts

[PHOTOJOURNALISTS TAPE OFF THEIR SPOT]
a writing through of through with you
semper presidential groins on coins
landscape call it what you wanna
i, with the lath of trojan hinden-guten,
do lower toy piano chimes to gurgling
literally they may
permit me to haze possibility
literat-ch-ch-ch-ch that's
brand spanking
or the maudlin crawl toward tenure ogle
cage's cheap imitation
shaves pavement between gaviota and galeta

[THE HEART BREAKS AND THE WORDS FALL IN]
scads goad
may i apply for another 'our'?
when we left
buster keaton's hat was flattened
the dial tone cognoscenti
fixture foreigner
picture all your
ars amatoria
spoken by a door
value is the sanskrit word for really very busy
old batryose and racemose
would ransom off her fan letters

[EDISON KILLED AN ELEPHANT WITH HIS HANDS]
nerf history saint get there timber fore
currently....
attest tomorrow

of breadth with dizziness in hieronymus kibosh isn't riveted
forced to smoke a menthol —uupp—there's dust on it
and the girls need their ephemera renewed?
pre-survive the crash by not scurrying
by divestiture a hired mime
of the punk cribbage byline
alternating and direct are
as your azure lecture circuit stud
where to go when the words no longer matter

camera feels up

buster keaton canola wrestles mary baker eddy
in her heart there is a malomar
some cinema per funnel

a ways away, to live among
eye-level anxiety (bob's big boy newton gingrich
blinks a match cut saphead)

americamera repair
i love you
but it's shiver me the chips keep shrinking

but nothing. show him your(e) cross
hurl a lightbulb through the beam
so to protest home-ageddon

my lover shook a leica
mal à junta of projection
unnerve, serve chilled with handcuff offering

this land is mylar
bert williams cold cream, madonna
preempting typhoon babs' grandeur

postcards of a gallows lens
a coccyx lens the lens that lends us promo balm
the settlers said *how,* too

mcveggie burger lenny bruce
lenny bruce three tablets free
i am pop because of dervish leeches
your mother castrated that astronaut on the today show so politely
it's lenny bruce who licks his astroontological piles
lenny being capable of criticizing me
while the confines dine on the doted
the culture stole the masterpieces without pondering the market
next year's lenny bruce is silvern
i say let the vietnam deniers write their blyric eyewool
fine, fine (louie, louie) a bust of lenny bruce in
blue recycled hand dyed exit polling ('atta) data
at once entirely of petit fours
another clumsy tooth fairy , another
orpheus and other stories
another world another world another you another you
lenny bruise, it is said, didn't "get" meltdown
instead (here it comes!)
                    darkument
anyway the i-bomb merely deaccesorized, so go ahead an' croon
how about badly designed and boring?
how about gladly bending for el benny loose's
trumped up chump change
bristling from the edgar hoover memorial vacuudemic contrabas-
soon?
cable, coddle, fatal diaper thrive
hating hating you, lenny bruce is
he who sues the dust and settles
leveling againstness kisses, this is
lenny bruce's yahtzee noose
off signing

**"i'm dead. thank god it's not
emotional here."**

—*Bernadette Mayer*

1st day wearing Lathe
sicko notices a nurse shark in his muse stuff
hair light gerundive daylight hazing time
the time is since

1st day expectation candlepins
seize your money maker
while you microphone the blue
roosevelt ate aloe

1st day since "the original gorilla"
my love is 2 BR APT
i can not have her standing
the people of sao paolo and my dance of prowess

1st day speaking to someone
the scrollwork on the casket, cover,
bake under jewish pthooey and media tainted caribou meat
he has literally come out of the little end of his own horn

1st day with pink post-it blinkers
to have settled for a bi-borough quarantine
my lover jammed a peso in my paw
there is no free trade in heaven

1st day unduly
either i feel faint or apes ape paving
i love you anapest as opposed to
the lone ranger loaning tonto to his ghost

i thee

it's early in the oddening
to be this late in the staggering
to be i thee armed and maimed
with eight waitlisted braille declarations

i thee keeps us off the streets
the ringbearer's armed and maimed
wherewithtwenty, wherewithfour
the only word left was *lest*

i thee cower lino orlon blob
it's early in the wrinkling
i taste you and not appropriations bill
i thee body fluid toxins and car service sergeants' arms

human come with kilo of plums
i thee rid sir ceremoaning opal
serin-owning om in hornetted corsage
on i thee drip from the mess to the head

hair
a replica of the deceased in aspic
i do groom the sect's crick
right through i thee one large tear

the i thee fire me grow trust-according lampreys
last place at consummate annulling
i thee i thee needing time
the parasites who feed off cake

dedication

to the hums, low and ho
who have pratickally taked up singing

to the uncommercial mulberry:
i whine white pearl bluster

to we should be so lucky
while groucho's FBI file, #100-407258, states
the united snakes

to pandorable

"gadthookth"
                    —*Céline*

to the law firm of deep throat now a countron
"is it ever hard to criminalize floatation..."
to own thine
to buy for
to orderlies with foaming hypos after
gangs of aphorists

the uvulas of influences
a three-y and-a
without whom no
codexes amass markets (as per in...)

nerve of
a version
to tee on
to being finished reading

office rocker

sun pool on tape spool loop
loupe the rule purling plural
you, cruella, have reached your keeper's incremental lintbrush
if freedom's pigeons
when and essen with three equals
if the right to hate to bear this chest-high niceness
this franca-phony not another hi, hon
elevator don'taskstration,
the day, harrumphing, i swear, "sirs"
stapled it flaccid to the desk
colleagues under see it
tweezed into inboxist pinhead horded hills
don't negotiate or glow
learned tourniquet carpet
like slobber to a dog
like increments and excrements
all your hard work will soon pay off

no livsies

raga flying fiskars
rhome is where the do as's
study metallurgy by organizing miners

i am in love with the back of the fridge

which shows its show of hand bones
almost without will

which breath on tacky two-face paint
incites manhattan island maiden tenant pharmacists-in-
waiting how to stare at plates of friskies

downstairs gary gray eyes

three-sixty clowns and picadors and the bull is inner dimly

this is a caravan poem availing auctions of effects

entertainment as oppression versus war is a stimulus

refrigerated tresses larmes of an armchair cherry

dear god,
next to the mustard

precinct

for Thalia Field

means [muffled sound] to [form of banishment]
sitting on an oscilloscope
on grand and [ways god's camp]
ladder to the gallerists' red devil jigger filled
collectable gas
on one [idea is this?] boulevardier escape key
the guns become [famous waistlines]
the [lie there] hike their
geiger green ticonderoga pencil foil awfully bold
shown to house [something between rare and rampant] can
[drug vogue] discarded bucket seats be
prosecutorial?
hospital exhaust grosses/crosses/gooses
the gag vomit, pepper sucker, shake buzzer [vent a novelty] district
flush shaken
with the gin of division

counter chickens

ok who can
bottomless?
my larva's sore from gary snyder-paintball in the parking limn

why the conflicted hurl bibs
i dream dreamily and mishear, will
this still fresh fixation
crystallize or candy?
need deep knee bends? intoned the gofer

it was a shell in mamaroneck
the stutterers like grunion
wave air into the theory we're
all high off aerosol

leave for work under fingernails and burning
the all clear nuclear family boom
chuggalugga come in bunches
what you, ya big lug, lug
fits in the thumbhole of a bottomless inky mug

loss of halving hard of braving
ball faced big beleaguer fixes to sphinxify his
best of
pint to bite sized
pork or rubber scorpions

you know the limitsky's?
collecting *kind of* can be profitable to the sued
as in regular laramie where
litigants meet at king kullen
to barter model lark

i lost half my
medieval anesthesia during bertha
the rain played
"water that's hot"
while snuffy loaded figurines into the breeches buoy

loss of canada dry
a crenshaw and a hand and
jansenist ironware, basically
these vintage crush cans
didn't they use squid ink?

ill hale postcard of parking lot appraisal
this is cause for undeveloped rolls
the breaded hordes
diming on a burnished treasuredness
take it anymore

date unknown (a.m.)

no sleep for you,
scoliotic wholesome-wrecker
a bad xerox of why
honesty with loss

if you can't say anything...
stroke, stroke, stroke

i am a shame, with dogtags

these three lazaruses
give up all at once

plutonium core, keep reading,
because my dinah might
change no's diapers in this line of plying

to give yourself the finger requires flexibility
or misinterpretation
i'm known on my knees

why do i bother, boy do i whoa there
relationship of whites to yolks:
the credits crumble holbein's buying spree

love's logos glossed

my love's
logo—the drool on somalia
knock it try it china doll
genetic photographic lick—is
scripted in lao: *drink me*
beneath languet fronds of
potted doom palms potted
doom palms potted [ahem]

this logo is a corrugated [ahem]
the type used is
no point
one of the guys
my love it's told sold
socialist revolution phone cards
so nobody boils over anymore
be with freeze it's eat crow shit crow
no one cares the wires show
she likes
vestibules and that's my weakness now

big chair photo

carnival askew
with the hudson too cyan
my whole family is alive (8:26 pm)
order in limp lime popsicle prophe-cc:
ambition zagreb onion rings
blanked on homonym, midwestern
crassness of a
twistoff cap put back
painted hot rod flame, as a race
le rayon vert and skaters
swill a hill of
hope is kinky at the fairgrounds in kankakee
cutting room dixie cup kinkier (and solid state)
what the federals spent on equals signs in
dix-huit cent soixante-six
most everyone i know is reachable
forget my weight and age
do you guess i can recite in Fried, the uncle tongue,
and look past the mcdonaldization of rabelais
toward donner party parking
livestock like the fright wig on a dime

prompter ordinal

fudgegate synthesizer privacy
why wait
texas continues to be texaco, frank
plus the bigamists—
think copies of *nize baby* rained on said school board indoors
next mess: undid givens
the mental health system heaves a collective preventative
thanatos on toast
shinola's latest, labor equals methadone,
is like water damaged wise men's gifts
a tinny inanity
where i grew up [fill in the banner]
zorro in a border skirmish circle ®
read when to get reckless
and section *c* for how to reprioritize
(on the john with sword and ledger)
bide my
belied quote digitizing timecode
through sprocket holes now's the
next guy's scheduling wet dream
bird'd turn
78 (with bronco nagursky)
it all operates retaliatorily
by it—breathe—i mean
there is a will, and there is a way:
don't conflate them

former republics of
cashiers i have loved

codpiece swimmingly
poem written in an elevator

making the next light
traffic and weather together

as antiques, blues,
rotisserie, shoe repair

dial-a pile-a
here i

reap evolution's remaindered custard
drop a dime and pick it up with

training—a fake
would play like bit-o-honey springtime

abort shrift—stuck in your head
automa ton of

subtlety excuse, i
cater, no, wait

no, passive was declared a
mood trulyly

wore my best googol

to peoplease you

ironized brontës
(or burl ives's) enlivening

by being bored of, of course
crimes for

dear o
in a low moan—crow over
rank and life'll heil "policy wheel"
smile while
swallowing a spool
whadda they make
the scratch-off card coating out of ?
—on accounta
it resembles lead

sun meals sepal priests, car of fad
dashboard for schtup a ornamental yucca
monday the grooves in the side of dimes
score, calla lily lolly, an angle on cargo
misfit security guard epaulettes of polyesteryear
are here we go again the mere mention
contains corn syrup

is with us here
is über for a few, felled
as a seclarity guard
reaching for his carrot stick of riches
pop, you're
secure sucker
an ardor for flushing, darl'
suss cess stay
soused on fangoso lagoons,
daily cream of frangipani leis, i
dream of fiji & company

restrung numbers racket with
fat cat gut

napoleonly

i hate a history of plumbing the way a gay pastry thinks it's broccoli rabe
let her hate the who cares exclamation point chummy bunt pan trundle
the suck a frozen sara lee subset of merger humor
the rays say albert finney and anouk aimee
tad-a-minute have halves the little things mean the mediocrity festival
the giantess figurine i told this story already on auto-pylon
statue of liberty play with dilbert's sonnets just add milk to shims
thomas nast as a brash crash test ten times fast
son is this your bißt iron new wrinkle
multiply fie by five and there's my
hi mom and rainbow afro wig
kegger, jillionth pinnacle, we netted an akin down near the color print
incentive-to-dither-gram john 3:14 on petrarchan vietnam
why be *beep* when we can
get under hood with angelfood filter
the collected word bubbles of ellipses is it unelectorate to stare back blank
canada dry flint bisque tijuana cheap
thrill me through breeze and sheen and shrimp in peach
like sand through the hourglass
to die with your name on something flaky

annul in the family manx act
sixty years ago
ergo this filler
that lactating cat, kerouac,
laid the state against expenses
brillo jello (& now gentlefallow las
cinquentas son las trentas
on a paranoiac color wheel, *jai*
windshield wipers

sandbox panzer division change at jamaica
hey is for intercourse
mama are we
praved?
oedipus vitreous schmata business dentist:
where zeppo marx and sammy davis jr. share a sauna
carved of *ever-after piechart-topping*
quarter-in-a-feedbag weighted no way deign delay
the sky's the
sky's business, here's why

paw-paws smell of vomit and so's my face
the laws say
no little pie in lobster's kisser
comedy fit to schfrint
down to one can dinty moore, frosted
caked cables, a gray azalea, less
silver tot finder sticker (that's what they all say)
how goes the slather of emollients?

well the world cup is hitching off without a goal
can you name sorts of stoppage?
mow the neighbors' locusts, local
television presenters croak
presently, li'l ole satellite dish installation AK
47A—vote
your pleasure cruise credit oodles
dude screwed up the solstice
locking the keys in it

all for one woofer
drive everywhere over (skews
me) serving finger (fuck) foods to
"the truly..."
members of the julep
club that would have me feeding
time its
sow's ear diamond chip rolly poly load ups
so sore bone the bozo nose-o
crashes to the floor
however well fed, well, time was anorexic

privalléged

old bars of soap [see: freedom]
visit ophthamollusc wishes his
wishy washy lenses on a triscuit
[the kicker] cycles of binge and jitter
get in the way mate
have folksong, nil; have gare du nord, portable
that'll learn ya
i am pehfectly well aware of what i prefeh
and what i do not prefeh
search on 'uppity'
the peoples' squeakling weeky reports
the postal service going public
arose is
a color glasses
everyone is pro-prune except the juniper
and he awoke one day a franchisee
skilled in the arts of hafta gotta and needa
and mostly all there
a new model sport utility
blaring through some anemone'd setting
with a brick on the accelerator—click!
of all the puns on *a crust of bread and such*
horde my stock in billie holiday
i am sweating a lot of annual reports by now
save now
i was forced to believe in troves

emulsion number

how do i stay trained on?
casa del leaden
i've been thinking
on the sunny side, *cheep*; on the dark side, *coo*
these your minutes?
my average voice can't chant arabe
though i'm sleeping with the tapes
and yesterday a meter reader
said homeless tapirs snuzzle puzzle pieces off the street
the golden bowling scoresheet orgy—oil of loyal synths
sinks a second folka-rocka-boom
as earnest weekley reads me *locate, collate, kill* his
sand wedge to buboes of just do it
an epidemiology of your name on my parade—fade to crates
malted maypo glazed in disappearing ink
i dream of v-ger and its cheap
deep image body mist
see here, seer, sir...[eyebrows raised]
there is the additional depth charge we mentioned

rip van revisited

a tuba band works its
junk into antique junta

the barges on the *no duh* river
thick with original cast jesus christ superstar soundtracks

chance of showers it turns out
soybean magnates outside lubbock
have agreed to purchase our treated feces
err's roadhouse hosts its
sixth six minute symposium on the aesthetics of rust

and as for ken doll arms and aphids
there've been much less pleasant pancake breakfasts

if ya shan't inherit, ya can't disown
—show manolo the anthrax popsicle, connie
though i couldn't get the *soy cubano, soy popular*
mask on my face to stay

how do our voters grow those
mock orange municipal shallow yellow ribbons
left over from DESERT SHILL so well?

the man in the mascot's hot;
a departed shrike has been captured at the crag

and chasm insurance [a (la) lasting peace]
the mayor may not "leather vehicular interior"

what lollies in the mouths of pre-swallowed mottoes
a place to grow old (and be shown)

domestic bliss album

first exhibition of moving pictures in kittentown
post polio
but bumblebees chew up the patio
but cross a shuttlecock
one peeved christendom for schoolboard
fishing village; artists colony; speed trap;
                              last bid gaza strip
ukulele pasta boil; ahoy a
                    cause
foxes flee in lines and so are huntable from horses
counting colanders he wakes and rakes
before the three bean she will see to tend the lawn teeth
a lot of mail is glossy

is where we keep the warrantees

beneath the porch a shoreleave borzoi
a supermarket of generative in-jokes
boss of the cock flavored soup mix is zen-like and supply-and
tannic acid (f) of sex
who here rues the ant trap alas
root vegetables still and will lack cores
as all is viz
pumpernickel brunt
zvei for tea and structurally muck a muck, dear assessor
we're a couple of foam core doors

tiny diet politics

I (eek)
T (rex)
ID bowl man (see collective
anal retentive neilsen rating 1962-1999)
david duke, a german baudelaire,
the shoop in the
shoop-dee-*doop*-dee-doop, and
everyman (mandarin)—a prosthetic mensch
posit "walk into a bar"

claude debris-soufflé, in an essay
entitled "YOU JUST DON'T UNDERSTAND X TEN TO THE TENTH:
POPULAR MISCONCEPTIONS OF POPULAR MISCONCEPTIONS
IN THE SELF HELP LITERATURE OF IMMOLATION PUDGE"
notes "toads cause placebos"
get down on it an anthem candidate?
born under the sign of the line segment; the scarring of a ra-ra
nada

maybe a chemo of copy editing:
"think different~~ly~~" [P~~ICASSO~~, A~~L~~I, ~~EINSTEIN~~, ~~GHAND~~I,
~~MILES DAVIS~~]
mi mi mi *mi* mi mi me (e natural
e culpable pluribus
how come
        elysian John Grisham?
i see no reason
my bonnie loves my donkey
for if the world were only what ~~it~~ i~~s~~, brother
there would be no place for us

what me worry

1]

when lacan said "the ego is an inveigling"
dude musta blown $19.95 plus shipping and handling
on the same exact flobie i considered
an energy efficient way to look great on dates
identity is counterrevolutionary and anyway
lacan wore khakis
i try to wake up every morning and cockamamie show trial clearasil is
sacred?
but seriously, stereo...me...bought
i'd recommend revisiting your resumé or personal memoir
and if the powers that license *to be* to you permit,
inserting the hyphenated "rent-a" before a sampling of nouns
then recite it in the marketplace, ok?
o, don't think about it
invasion of the out of body zip drive ubiquities
remember william hurt afloat in tear-temperature liquid capital?
growing primitivist trivial hirsute about the titties?
it can't happen here
at least while telephones no longer have receivers
hello, my name is when it rings, i walk over to it and
let me ask the panel, might we be post-pavlovian?
you can't grow home again
mao modeled the stricter and harsher dicta of the cultural revolution on
pirated scripts of U.S. sitcoms
that's *us* sitcoms
did you know one of buddy holly's crickets wrote the theme to
mary tyler moore? wow!
but really,
are you an ethnic or a specialist (oprah needs to know)

2]

when i think of identity and innovation,
dumbo choked on his very own snout
"onanist myself
pretentious true one" writes brian kim stefans (according to the
hyundai blimp)
"i'm the business section" writes brian kim stefans
(according to the tax dollars used to lure the stock exchange to jersey city)
"at least i can stand my own two knees"
writes hung q. tu
(according to you,
dear friends, kennedys, and fellow aesthetic supporters, dear total cultural blackface incitees, fellow mold jones, dear returned and
deceased cola war veterans, target markets, assembled small press poetry lobby, dear www.queerrepublicans.com, dear shebang, dear
shebang shebang, dear white males against white whales, fellow
knee jerk back in the good old days when poetry was cheap damage
control team, dear dearly beloved and mandatory daily otherings, fellow hindenbergish gleaming gasbags, ladies and gentlemen of the society
for the denial of surface area, mr. and mrs. cusp of big crunch, the
people who brought you antonin artaud action figures, the poettasters
and the gobble selves, dr. and mrs., who are here today thanks to the
jeez, i'm jerky foundation: "clearing a space in the crowded commodity
culture for the auto-cannibal to have his fill," dear a suffocating
nation of nothing but poetry

—according to you

3]

single white male...umm....*I means lotions...I'm totally indepen-
dentist*...in a recent poem by tim davis (author of popey's up-

<u>-per arm</u> now unquotable due to legal squabbles),member of the
guild of collective, desperate unaffiliation
single local frontal globe sport labotomists of the glyph of the all-
meringue
single caspar weinberger buddha nature illegal flashcard traffic
single blunderbuss versus nanorobots
single latin scholar stuck with identity meaning sameness
single poetry chapbook released into orbit, rips through the hull of
a billion dollar space station, killing crew and timorous beekersful,
fucking hell, there's hope
single debtor—owes kim's video his firstborn, can't find *lust for life*
single white hawaiian triple negatives
single jewish when they come for the camps again hygienist or less
single poet with one lone tool: that'd be "star 69," think about it,
back-assed through the studly duststorm of miscommunications
that can't even stay missed, they'll speak to us no matter what we
see fit to slam shut

existential mon amour

i miss alienation
were cured rhubarb on
sincere langoustine
if alain delon's alfa gets hauled up
why do we stare hard at rebar?
it's 1961 do you know what our very valent
flickering atomique fille be thinking?
the lens-all here; putt politburo bennetton
every time yuri andropov's dog dot
                    dot dot
it's owl's job to
smear up the office of the self-represented
and when i told the foreman how an
anarchist might talley ballots with his hands
a gleam in his said *sensitivity training*
great crepes of shame just
me against a gujarati A-bomb
chairlegs go gastrointestinal hi, i trade head
if you click on sisyphus' balls
your debit card can come into relation with ordet

in 1998 there continued to be shipping
(think of zoos) or israel was thirstier

i earned, let's say *copious* euros
writing survey questions whether any
schoolchildren remembered what *counterrevolutionary* meant

and remember us or them?
eye ear nose and hope and
ire noise and hype
and all was scatigetical
were the pureblood to fake another scene change

we thought *political nutrition? lick the brecht stamp!*
but it proved self-adhesive
naturally finally slipped from the adverbial best sellery

in 1998 napoleon and michael eisner...
and my aunt in patchogue's cereal box awarded her the eastern star
is why they put pockets on the pocket t's
—to accommodate another croix de guerre

think tokenly, act loco-ly
the commemorative memorial millennium pewter minted hill of
beans

the registered trademark sun up
as was crass master balalaikaists,
customer secret service agents
desiring a certain loaf
momma's boy by the mogadishu beach

in 1998 i'm here affixing *aww* to the lazy lids of the statue of *shucks*
johnny institutionalization-seed, light and breezy to the core, is
calling yessirreal "sino-idol worship" viz
selective focus in those *drill holes in parole* fantasy camp ads

the last drop of good
coffee fields have no odor tour t-shirts
a critique of pure
        prices but i *can't* pay
m y h e r o
look for the can in the plain brown can (trappings
but you *must*
        up grown mountain
of sprouts in east side windowboxes
"go doo-doo, schultz" a failed
facelift entreats her afghan ex post starbucks
a culture and its regularity (colon)
why i'm heightened (slash)
national pastime playing pocketpool
up goodnews clumps of uppers
        i was on the treadmill when it come to me,
'cappuccino' meaning 'hooded?' only half a
caput mortuum? you tip them or their fangs—
same old maniamanes...chipped
cup enough con leche nuts
the french are on anti-depressants
psychoanalysis boite's been lost
today's tahitians feed gaugin spam
    jog forward, derivistes
glory nescafe in a filtered headwind

pooled blood in mario puzo font, you've
alluded to it, turning on a dime by sucking FDR
the nth art is stuporimposition

joe schnorkeled a schistosome
plus his *you fuckin talkin to me?* routine
to the buffleheaded drive-thru menu
—and otherwise mute as an NGO with agida

hallelujah, you beautiful mixoploid city, type quintuple A,
maxed-out hell hound can't afford a dog that
shits blue is sooo "older sister"

according to a bass-y PhD the UN wants bullets;
three bullets recommending what to do when azerbaizhanis bite
finally 'sanity' the way the sun oil company'd sign it:
besame blue on a well-whisked yellow batwing
crimes against el fillerup drive us to drive, prides of a pyre, i
nourish nounish embargoes

a snifter of quik and back on 95-nowhat
further the urban renewal fungus shafts of lesser new england's cap-
itals
—well, you're culpably right
kipling called the planning commision fuzzy wuzzy
and then let them eat real estate
have you seen a lop-
eared economy teeter?

indicators thank a
shakey's animatronic kodiak might get real chummy
with a stamford glass clamboat full of mutual fund shepherdess'

POW fetishist piñata emptied of incentivistic groats?
answer talentlessly please, you've
topped up the hovercraft it's
life beneath the off-ramp
doesn't glug

the death of alexis

for A.G.S., R.I.P.

far as you can listen, songbirds
i'll bow a barcode on a migratory tongue
the goddamned
things that do grow

she'd dreamed she'd harmed a jain, she'd
spilt toxins on the U.S.S. mcsicklecell
she'd
looked up
random and found the old french *suddenly,*
violently from *a blow from the edge of a shield*

all her life she thought *alexis* meant
without speech when
actually-contractually-i'm-
milking-the-brick-wall-of-purpose-to-be-on
it means to ward off
or meant it
an alexiteric is an antidote, no?

so,
bones about it
it's the saturday since and still no pigeons
the megalopolis' grackles have gone somewhere
to listen to G BIV
—but the light sounds vacant
everyhow she sang we're flightless
screaming open-beaked

touch: a grippe, a rigor
the white noise machine is buff and rough and tough enough
meantime i find i'm eyeing

supposing the goyim of sheboygan nudge their remington micro-
processors to *on*
the lamplighter's wrist action launched a thousand shifts
tribally, a key in a slot

land of the clap hands lamps is redux, duhhh
see to it mr. sprocketeer punches in his calorie count proper
make your own & julio gallo spin cycle cowtowns

as fudgie remembers the hydraulic ram
he knuckles up all jesus ex machina
finger foods please a beleaguered flick-o-crat
matter of digitalis i am delightfulness to met you
what's on up in over between us?

does a drubbing? (battened down hands on)
keyboardists forage yeast in the awning of a one
                        think it done

peel me these boy in a bubble franchisees
KLONDIKE 5, you lock the lock
you blank genie blink
like a chain reaction and it ain't somebody sneezin in china, i tell
ya
our leader's finger on the watermelon seed

pressed ham, cellular one
and when it's raining i don't miss the sun

the natives have a fax machine (the sound of one boing clashing)
son of sort of purportive orchid of submission, or of stamped, self-
addressed english only *je ne*
         the tennessee waltz
         on a best hits cassette
         that's been left
         in the cab
         of a semi
i try to remember that during sex it helps to talk about ex presi-
dents
there is an eturnkeyity of predigested meat
what boys call soluble saccharin while they're feeling philadelphia
giving enriched rice and the gecko meat of startup
the natives have graphics and
am i right in remembering a candybar called 'payday'?

let it be a
hatha of "i m - p o r t......e x - p o r t......"
while the senator is busy aping our aborted savior,
we on this side of the aisle are putting chives on a candied chicken
and pondering what else it is that charlie don't
who wills the watch fob bill, i am an elected looter
lobster dinner with the DNC and CREEP (note:
bring both bibs)
but turtledoves are furrier making the world safe for the stock exchange
hatha half a hafta
imperative to prone, where's *my* deep throat:
lickerish meaning eager
a poll-y glow of creeds peppering and seeding the hard hard roll of
tortoise paced speedsters
asqueradingmay as the state

snaffling-lay a poppa doc, a jujube, two sprites
akin to birth of napoleonic biopic
world of miracles and voiceovers
put past me please pass me
a schoolteachery iodine stain
—welcome to smear dab cinemas, heck
prosopic means pertaining to the face
must d-ration hands after using the full frontal room
color me obvious a carpet
where the bared skin rug was
can you do dressage in your undershirt?
an hour to go and the head on this big gulp still ethanol
our founder had a tenor to shatter pyrex
the kurds: a single issue like affirmative servitude
take this brother may it
flutter cinematographically
today is
on purpose; on, blitzen, dress a squad of
politically erect extras before the credits furl
western x disease provided by
one big union
how many avalanches do you have? canned
howling of aardwolves? assortofness
owing to mao's dimple: make up! and kiss
comes a sequel-begging end
the white(wash)man in the bear suit wilts
our stalins are only human
sprinkle foibles onto press inking linking dinka-do
truth in "avert eyes-ing" o my
mediocrity
is true too

retroaddictive casheroo
me dreams be good for me
(at least as much as i will finally see
prisoners what washing dishes with their semen)
in norway they appreciate kinetic cotyledons
a whole dacha devoted to my manitoba phonebook ruse
more kirsch!
every critic in oslo got it
when i conflated oscellated blenny with the blessed damozel
or like teetering kippers they flopped to the firetraps,
cubbies painted habitué
and housed with nooks and sideboards hosting tempters:
a blowtorch a marlboro and a brillo box of cereal called "asbesto's"
or better
a synchronous converter and a synchronous condenser
all hooked to a synchroscope
beneath three tureens of cider, hot and hard
lard mind!
up where water curdles
per art per dumpling blur
they don't know alpo from mignon but it
rewords golden average apples
a file on a lifetime in a studio amounts to oh, an
apt palaver
come inhabit
hate rooms with calartsy arc welding hobby horse
stand in the way of canvasses embarrassed to just be so
so they animatronically jiggle
crock of endive sponsored by the K of C, that's
"Kind of Conceptual"

in "part of parcel" you mail yourself a mauser
getting hold of lillehammer's post office was a
sunday sardine (as they say)
but those strident gun laws! lucky my assistant
can say "imitation" in six languages

dear ma i went west with the shipped off flats
dear jerry is the institüt insured?
dear dr. aski, transfer my sessions to my son
(and ignore the bandanna, it's mine from 'nam)
lamb with berries and a snifter of seal urine
is this fêted?
a TV in every gallery, OK
i get it
heartbeat and hardy har compete in a global
marketplace of shorted pacemakers
dear son, they're
wild for leonard cohen here

CHECK ONE

☐ hotel   ☐solution pressure
        ☐ a halvelings hams

YES OR NO

are columns capitalist? are dreamers
irrotational? it
rain on carcass floor?
christ of the andes cast from an argentine cannon?
would you call 'screw' low dutch?

CHECK ONE

☐ maybe   ☐pedantocracy   ☐overpoll
        ☐overvote   ☐the diminishing niches
☐buntpans to class   ☐which nasty?   ☐get the guest
    ☐inhale information   ☐2 plus 2 ruses   ☐spoonsful of burgoo

TRUE OR FALSE

the morning seemed to herald a glorious day
i told my dentist all this
who am i
it all began just like that
thomas sat down and looked at the sea

SHORT ANSWER

NEWS CASE WHEN UP FLIES a rixy. louisa sidearm leaves sunstricken with the typeface's serifs strapped backwards to her robinet. there will be no mug of seenie bean drunk on deck while kurt st. roch steers the caledonia toward the roaring forties, no hub of cob money brought up, no priceless ponce de leon-era porcelain decelerometer. instead the tumble-trudge like an ex-president-elect past the quaint-forsaken outskirts of sunstricken, treatise on fu-hsi left—finished but for the dotting of the t's—sitting in her public housing project kitchen nook, her skeleton of a glyptodon and months worth of relaxers just prescribed abandoned to teenage scavengers.
why is louisa afeared of the inventor of thermometers?

YES OR NO

did woodrow wilson pursue a policy of 'watchful waiting'?
did woodrow wilson reject a policy of 'dollar diplomacy'?
the relater goes cluck?
is the tree medic a tree? the tree of chastity a cactus?
would you call self-help endarchical?
how about westchester neutral ground?

CHECK ONE
☐ normal succinct acid ☐ normal syllable ☐ normal school ☐ normal honey ☐ normal forest ☐ normal dropper ☐ normal fault

disgust como....?
a poet goes—listen to the thespian parentheses nest)
"this actually happened," one who is the high road
sits a spell
does it therefore cease to be a chameleon?
it was my job most mornings to start 'the ropes'
quote, "woke the ropes"
discussed *Coma*
the set of shower and euthanasia chromed
blue in the proof, the outfielder
broke stride the more i spoke
like a wild bill hickock lighter,
linoleum of resistance
...i think it was two halves,
yeah, definitely, two halves
--study toward a PhD: AUTO EROTIC
ASPHINXIATION: Contemporary Poets
Still Pop Bitter Pills of *THIS*
all decay is quaint—soldat
on my knee, 'tis
at cost, this
landscape with woman and antipodes
not even (not odd) budgeted, she flew fuit
the more she parlez-vous'd it

desert riot
over steno pad (cried for an hour
took in a 'flict)
perhaps the most assassin-proof novelists plot covert ops on rather
dan, rather
dung beetle me
official oval office set of scimitar coffee stirrers
the gods must be standing again
aw,
reelect a creepy daisy (old saw)
see under "cryomicrophone" this is
ezra pound
reporting from bahrain (titles,
logo, plague of lenses
ice cream break on the U.S.S.
IROQUOIS CONFEDERACY
we are lurid and assured
tippecanoe and the economy stupid
try these
new laurels, *gulpf*
fire when furled
own riot, own nosecone,
sown soporific biologic cumstain scud
the danger's in refrigerators

history pimps itself it
depletes itself i say
history is a selfmade man—and worships its creator
history hanged itself to avoid the daily task of dressing
like mackerel by moonlight it
shines and stinks
        [germany sent seven thousand gasmasks to israel today]
history is a despotism tempered by epigrams
there is no other granola like this
on the board of *who am i* incorporated sits
lists deposed by history's inquisitors
times you've yelled you whoreson zed
times it befell the three little sows
trade in houses for hotels and
heft the rent
        [flying tigers]
why should men eat shrimps and avoid cockroaches
methodology of the fucker   [flying
      tigers]
history is the worship of jackals by jackasses
pickle-herring in the puppet show of history
say *steering clear*—all arks are off
nobody can beam and warble while
chewing pressed history and diabolical mustard
fresh baby cranium peelback [context]
dust on the saga
basta

"oops, perhaps
i've written this"

—Stephen Hoagie

to photograph it is
too ms. kubilick
here we see a wrenching
east european dream archive scene
[grips card light toward infinite regress set]
say *l'état* the day a
"poets" to a grumpy one
succumbed to parcheesiing the terms

"marrying" ketchup bottles, for instance (for tips) become
"alterity's suture"
and all i got was these lousy terms
"swings his axe at the virgin turgid"
to playing with a discourse deck!
here we see a barrel full of
strips of exposed positives

honestly i miss hash
the fact that at denny's the food looks like the photographs
dream in which i am forced to propose an experimental confession-
alism
president suharto, a pumpkin
in autumn, the majority of pumpkin
in poetry it's open season
MY EDUCATION: A MATCHBOOK BACK
tock! ok, ok, "au-*teur*"
style larder
the gun bearers raised their quotes"
"i'm back and i'm perhaps"

law-mart antigen

my reflection in the barrette, state
cougar, everybody conflate
swordfight with pack of mango
guerrilla registration the enquirer insists
gandhi diet!
lime in it

zonked college try
the transitive waiting, warring
ghosts with hosesnips
it's like the 26th of july in aisle nine

it's real manager fur
we're all pledges in this
fraternalistic competitiveness bless-a-thon
the counters blindly check-out
past the pommel horses there where it's indivisible and livid

one last mini-snickers
will this vorpal trip the ringer?
a rival gang of orange julius clerks
found the corpse of the alleged "commandante del'arte"
in among the hip waiders perked to death

too much poetry not enough snow
~or~
manifestoes don't have colons

for Stephen Rodefer

i'll take mental health refugee with kalliope accompaniment ~or~
ornamental cabbage addict for 200 talents, jack
in love with an actual hole punch; a fragmented gas
when i grow up (keep looking shocked)
i want to be a principal or caterpillar

the foggiest speaks: my baggy! i signed for these!
garbled speaks it's
unseasonably...something
harm maybe,
or *wiled*
why did the american government hire ingrid bergman?
anyway the body hasn't ceased to breed
speaks a nice vitalized most favored inveigling
top of the maggot to you, kicking a dead koalatics

more chains than keys—the cinema isn't all that doesn't cry for us
je sais à quoi tu penses
and look, bub,
cut guzzling the subtitles i sub
(mit) _{one} harlequin to a vicious lesser than
antsy nostalgia for manson
ha ha ha ha osiris by way of pelting
now is the winter of our content

a cogito ergo moment

The author of *Dwell* and I discuss life works. He with a 2/9 smirk, and I with a nearly 11/21. He removes a copy of *A* off the shelves of the author of *Ameresque* and the author of *Rx*, who are currently on the west coast, being showered by the Jews of Malibu, and giving a reading before the sundry Francophilia of San Francisco. The copy of *A* looks like a chicken leg in the beak of a black-capped chickadee, held by author of *Dwell*. The night before, in a bar that specializes in Ratner's onion rolls and martinis rimmed with Tang, he has misheard 'über alles' as 'braless,' and made frequent mention of the "bisexual Canadian lifestyle." The bar is filled with fashion industry slag, and no one understands me when I say "my other son's a dock-tah," and misunderstanding, they seem to want to tend to ask to photograph me. The author of *Dwell* mentions that the author of *Free Space Comix* has made the point that "with computers, you can write a life's work in an afternoon." Telling this story, the author of *Dwell*'s voice rings with approximately 29/50 of a sincere concern that we have devolved into a set of socialist one-liner writers. The author of *96 Tears* is giving a reading today, and the author of *Dwell* takes one of his titles off the same shelf the *A* came from, sampling a likely story. I am visiting the author of *Dwell* to borrow the author of *Ameresque*'s tennis racquet. January is hardly tennis weather, but by calling the sport "Alpine Tennis" —invoking the spirit of the upcoming winter olympics in Nagano, Japan—I have persuaded two friends, the author of a history of exotic dancing, and a photographer with one leg of his tripod in the art world, another in the commercial, and the third plunged in the mud, to accompany me to the public courts underneath the west anchorage of the Williamsburg Bridge. I must confess that I will be missing the author of *96 Tears*'s reading, as a pot luck dinner party devoted to orange food follows the alpine tennis. I have composed a large molecular sculpture made of cheese doodles and toothpicks for the occasion. And as such, my life's work. Poetry is a weak force contributing to the molecular decay of my great, discrete, monolithic cheese doodle tower and alpine badminton tourney. I have a cat named "Steve," and regret terribly forgetting to mention to the *A*-bearing author of *Dwell* that the on-line NY Public Library catalog calls up two titles by the author of *I Don't Have Any Paper So Shut Up*. The other is *A Guide to Swaziland*.

**light bulb shopping (herr tortoise
wets his infertility allele)**

it's in the dictionary
look under *fragile*
lack the politics, clock licker,
to surface tense a bend in the dependable
we're talking two sorts of spree,
aren't we?
for whom the toll lulls, you may helm me indeed, feller, see
i feel like a specie
a high imperial type inclined to slobber on yon
glittery daikon and screw it up and in
coincidences is last stand at and
information missile died at bend in glass
[anything plus calvinism] was made to be broken
has a fang hanging out
triple vapid glory coil
for transistor's silver
i baked a mistakes-were-made
squeeged up the vigor tube, too
i feel like a jolly giant's lost wallet
hurtling down onto farms and fields and fixtures

solid potato salad

serve up some of that skin, soldier
while me and the boys bounce out
flinstone's ginseng meringue for hints a
sexusual fool's gold gloms the 'wanted' market

our friction's a throne
but we're begging boons and bones
simil-easy greazed fiddle-dee (with no pants on)
a waltz of the washerwomen orgasm stand in

(un)dressed as *Sacco-and,*
there is no accounting for the
state and i do mean we, we
Popular Rear will fall for what we believe

a circus peanut wrapped in the human flag
an odd little dance at word the president's pet's finished molting
oh, mixture winding sheet, do we
here have a pre-nup: "ban the atmosphere"

in snafoolery a beaut—
let me lick your toy ticker till it's
on the unparaded tip
always epic sniffles never *send me a tendency*

is vigor? yes and yes.
from one vampire to a vacuum pinhole,
how about a shot of out and out,
look at the size of my ear, pour it on

graham, whose alias is
opening his junkmail delicately
"like a botched circumcision"
there's more drama in the audience
they tear open the televeezor
and find it filled with silt and ipecac
—and unstable andirons, molto grosso,
huminah amigo, the limitless embarrassment
it appears there's a haggis on my desk
calming batman language of animation
will sit four thighs forward
for the man is mad at the otters channel
—disney shotgunning otters
on laudanum and an ill physical pickle
i mean the real world is three-legged-
dog-dash-one-armed-woman land and
"a good spot to pick somebody off"
let's stick to screen font imponderables
beneath the snow is old snow
defined by lack of leisure
private citizen with control of clicker
remembers rosey ring
lolling down the grapefruit seed extract aisle
humming meta- anything is trite
you gotta fight
having took apart the onion and the trumpet
define overtime

planet of look good every day

styrocam, yamcam, snowmancam,
lyricam, cancam, federal identity
o sweet annulvio do go and seek
a badly edited news program promo
nougat and endorphin flavored
amateur director cataract
the media r us, gloss
on gloss homestead
instead of writing this i am
refinishing

gristmas

de rigeur gregorian
louis the technique
today, divide
shinolauthority, a ray on
yon ghoulee myrrhburger
maybe no double-zero leap year
to pander to toshiro mfune being chimneyless
grin and agitate it
mom is in the kitcheninny
welding gelding cookie cutters till they're
deform-friendly
the family flak jacket out and
handy
and tantamount to silently communicating
mit der aliens in der distant mist
hail the crockpot dial and the light
stays on!

cash cow slaughterhouse

the gift of
fellow 1997 diaperers
sorry, we're open dilapidates the whitmanic
any tandoori can-do attitude
looking awfully like a countdown

that's one chunnel, six abandoned
executive office blocks
the takemitsu cassingle and a balsa melon baller?
with your purchase,
a free gentrification of the kirghiz
a speedo for the bloated corpse
do you take sans?

mile high side order
cost of divvying increase, cop,
andante, cop
this is not to criticize
everyone has their project mongoose
are these your turkish missiles, sir, a purgative
giving way the sealtest trade winds
the bell atlantic winter solstice
nike dada
reach way back and opt

invective against swan song

for the proctologist's daughter

academus told me where you had hidden helen
though i think what lacquers us more mirror blackly than the greeks
is our bubbling inadaptability and frank resent
we need transition team to get *gone fishin'* sign turned
somewhat frontal
though go on oprah, gastropod, and excorsize by being paid is
practically the sayeth,

               acting's taxing
after lawyer glow there's therapy and ovens
john wayne bobbit's looking for a job
and i guess i admit how pain is syntax, radical
anyway, i'll always hate you for the way you've treated me
a smear of lyric poets, being lonely,
has escaped from a lab not unlike your

        compassion, timing, aim
             why not ask them

**Davis: what else is there besides
identity?
Fagin: all types of birds**

air hostess (1933) true to form
and muscilaged to content
fennel on the playing field
out of left [brain, wing, overstimulation] *select one*
the studio's chessboard packed with bishops
the heart is [oh, stop it] a historicized brave new template
stamp! love thy commodifier!
give me newsreels of bombardiers or
barnstormers' *sturm und*
eventually Pakistani A will hide in the wheelwell
and get to heathrow untenably alive
aw hell, all i write is couplets

if the details set us free, "where's the *ball and*?"
eventually guides strew marble chips around athena nike
furious love with the same old same old enclave:
"parents, players, and fellow aesthetic supporters,
dagwood hugs his thought balloons"
in that way, fae wray's an ethnicity
that they could call it the great white way
that the buddha starred as "mickey individual"
in a number of low budget,
lusciously shot pre-code aeronautic co-
                                        optboilers
lordy, lift the fruitfly veil
the culture pitches us a treatment of the poverty of philosophy and
lordy larry, barring a big crunch sucking back up of lonely mr. monad
it might as well be us

the xanax of influence 2:
MacWellmanUncleDaveMaconLewisHine

etherized to frothing
an asterisk indicates progressives sulk
ach, ghoulish skillet licker grown colloquial
this isn't blot out *hello my*
name is stickers union local one is it?
of piss and pissed which is abstraction?
the manatees are back filibustering propellers
hearing bing sing à la juke
gone the way of banjos into warships
ashcan cashcow
with that million dollar tennessee smile
lensgrinding fend for legislation
i loved a girl from downer's grove
the nays have place names
actor! cause! camera! aaaaaaannnd...
clawhammer pure act of zebrine stripe change
the folk music of industrialists, a social leerist's stomp
come glorify the pure products of america-a-go-go
blanche dubois was a
irradiated happy meal (and no minnie pearl)
never mentioned what *mencken* means
denken menschenaffe meaning anthropoid ape
the golf links lie so near the anthracite
(laugh) flash

the xanax of influence 1:
JohnGodfreyCharlesBernsteinAliAkhbarKhan

some threes. along these lines
ratner's frozen dinners. i'm
entrenching desayuno on
extinct flightless bird airlines
tiger bar, i'm craig, i'll be your corpuscle
the infinite elbowing of distribution
[loeb classical mandible, virtuoso killjoehill, under
cloak of loquitur]
in new jersey.......nothing this specific
the sun's gonna spongify
i, like brackets back to back
fire arrows like hellenic [clamber]
the old neighborhood still a kipper stripper
liberationist fire house string attached to c-note trick
old agnew
trick
east village trees some percentage crotch
melodious nape of pain if
miep gees was here a self of infinite density lemony freshening
a rhythmic cycle of
one hundred eighty five beats

smart poets society

for Dodie and Kevin

like ichthyology to fish
all my waterfalls
(coleridge'd
get a hard on at the cautley spout)
con carne schematis personae suss, brother
take limitless prescription and call me
in the heck aesthetics of theory morn
(rodrigo'd get a village rearguard hard on)
1-800-COLLECTIVISM side of fries
the body is (quickly, fill in "duck-billed raven")
a place for forest fires
if not full on fusion (tear it torrid)
the evisceratists
take on oakland at the oikos dome
tonight at ten to ten on the network of people's degrees
i sing of arms make the man, con-
ductrices of the mission brain pep dispensary
the spotsylvania grandmamas meet
bashbish louis althusser
in a spinal tap to the mat
—had a life but couldn't keep her

draw fire

seize the pane
able baker straight photography
lens backwards
is incidental the new the old
with their flying monkey oz wizard wings
a passive swallow
packages of flash cubes in der original Umschlag, die
Hülle, Decke, Verpackung,
sugarpummel dancing in their heads
in wisconsin, in the year of the unpunishable video blow ('92)
some salvation army saint claus arrested selling dope to homeless
a filmic flashcube dissolve to poof
snell backwards
there's a fishhook leavened in my lip
whole note halftone
windows and mirrors a SUNY dualism
iss kamera idea and so?
the instamatic doctor krino
turns from the world end quotes
to find a 1917 bank account of certain Zurich Ulyanov
still in the retina of escrow

bus station lozenge
a family-owned dictatorship of the secretariat a four wall
on the orskirts of own
i have four hours to strangle with a bag
and consider a slow drool to the potomac
or maybe rental, headlong, glare

los tubes nub their spectra down on
ask us damn, the sequel to the road to
a poet is on the drinking gourd talking about poets he knows
i have four hours to have the nerve net
larynx class action abandon
in hand to assure you, the vous-er, "there is:"

a) a biorhythm machine
kite tied to treadle potted
not silk and silken CO_2-atation agent like ragged gladiolas
a plastic exit rose and yes a grindstone

"the tusks, the tusks, that's not easy to say"
catheter ethnically marxes
i take my address to the knife sharpener
rub it and the return there
—poet still on phone—
hours past edifices poets he knows

western sieve

i went to see boogie nights but it was textureless
and three dollars to fix first gear personally
he's chinese is not a funny line
that's eight dollars to find
no one name a love child dziga in all of analgesic county
the following firsts and dirests
sink a caliper and ten coppers into smiley face phrenology
the birthday of a weapon, nullius fillius
nullibicity the odds better
i dropped ten dollars on the little guy
to deliver usufructuary hoagies to a wailing wall street
gigantic money tree the search for other rams besides the battering
i worked until i stopped is not a funny line, mean
time interns earn with the wolves
.79¢ on health food bon bon
sell buy sell by some odd (some aught) midwinter tube lit day
the waltz of the valley of the involved wallet
twelve buck a pop learn to crawl lessons
swim and hanker sink
i stood, then, in this kitchen
rented full of holes

love of bivalve,
imp realist,
corn pone encoder
frank in the bronx on a car phone
is another man's lumpen poison
a coney island of the bonded blonde
a ho-ho-kus of the luckiest
a sunnyside of the madagascar solution
just this k train, fifty
second street and lex of
testicular cancer in the bird in the hand
dry run in dinkinstown
an inwood of the head
a sinai a bellevue a
trade center synching us in
inflamed neighboring holdings
a rockefeller-purchased palisades
a random place upstate of the nates
home is where the votive no-holds smolder
my brother's hand in mine
headbutt pin number no time
to draw the blinds
fight songs syphon
power to the states' encephallic
blood-logged ever winking receiving team insignia
a free otherness with every pencil
graphite spine tap duke franz ferdinand's
nation building in love elixir
i hate your general manager
and the sky is clearer here

**egon schiele's copper pomegranate
& other stories**

last name unknown
but a lull
and we're separating salt from sugar with our tongues

just yesterday i presented my
ex with a winner's circle horseshoe of yellow mums
out and bought eyebright
you are made of ribbon
round zukofsky's catscan muzak

i am
crazy about you i feel
                    sick is
one from all
        {doze}

chapter spheres

in the gumball in decoration and all the moving parts *y*
is the night sky dark and not a screen of light
i've known he's who've lived off royalties
from ball bearings and eskimo pies
our teeth sunk in viet-ham
i'll see you in my genes, great grenadine alleles
sing you in my sthenes

it was winter not the underworld
red
knuckles
wondered

the decoy room

for Rob Santos

everything i see reminds me of something i can't remember
or can't tell how dr. burnahole's tongue feels
all the bad art per
capita can of
hypochondriac who can
lick his weight in police dogs strangles baby's glands

tomorrow will have funny knobs
the ones with rifles wake up near them
the big dig to piss in
a giottoized golden gamut halo
from "friends" treatment to
ripoff chocolate bunny trauma

now's the item
to run and holler from
see at first it was a craft that led to more dead birds
kinetic sculpture filled the pilgrims' bellies
four hundred falls of swinging chromium balls ago
go sit in your lebensraum or ten by ten den
and the dipper from the tinted window
of self expression and of
eight delights (including squid)

band together and blast the flash ray at canard
i'm telling you saying you—
this to you, son, because the weasel pit is a fine establishment
you can't spit without hitting a ten dollar hamburger
dick linseed is here—i get a shtick out of you, kid,
his son's named maceo or snake and
bakes bread in an ex particle accelerator

in here, smart ass, is the village of cheese
these boston people can't tell a rotted chopstick
from he latest issue of *mein sprach*
they take a date down to logan and claim they've got a bomb
a gotten gain (i hear ya)
renting out their hearts to summer people

anti-semitic poem
embedding loss
facsimile of pizmon
moses only had two books and
i self hate you love you
kaddishing at allen's shukhavati
your 258 organs and my one
this stale testament
billionth circumcision
sausage night, miss white
a song of waverly jamaica bay
hudson, healing and charming, jane
can not crystal "spend this"
night without you-ize
all for un
lest normative
a wrong turn at pizmo pun
i have
half a fascist in my
implicit honey honeycomb
memory or or my me, don't mind
having finally solved what i me today
Wir sind es noch immer

hole in hammer
a non-com list poem beginning with the climate
maybe i did write the simpsons
unfortunately my seatmate has a valid answer:
                    wave theory
a harpoon through two of us
i'd like to dedicate this song
against
to read
alle bahnen sind frei the day
che's bones come home
a walkman tattles: a little casket
police move along ten thousand viewers
the news with its *cut/choose*
you say 'ultimata'
every morning i'm 13th'd to death
toothpasted but a crock to put work in
a fresh batch of america balls
where no joke grows
unfit for bismuth
no ideas but in
tears for things

boudou saved from
kissing intellectual ante ass
the missus' maid just married a mute

—do you miss me?
    —la nuit, oui

it's my lunch hour so i
spit in the physiology of marriage

and meet kim for a teriyaki contents pageboy
we agree
poetry is a lay of wife
we raise the proletarian to a level of stupidity
attained by the bourgeoisie

i don't like soup ; i like boudou
saved from maquiladora hollywood remake

and gives the man a nickel to have to beg him for

it's my sardine so i
trade faded free trade treaties
the butler's clench hour did it it
seems is greazed
    yoke ye to yr keys
            —of loss of silent majority?

la nuit, oui

talkin' believe it to leave her blues

you lose yourself you reappear
and everyone is flu-y

talkin' eelshaped master/slave relationship
embellishment oink if you love jeez this is painful blues

bottoms up and out; ubiquitous bottoms
friendly with the floor
the poorest, spectrally,
are ROY, G, B, and I
calculate vestibulesful of light, set pelvis deficit
you don't hear the word toil

talkin' showjumping empty ant farm eat it with wrapper on
box bottom chelsea's gone (and socks?)no stuff but in things
and a separate fountain for everyone is outsourced segregation
trueblood blueblood sugarpops at last she's gone
able bodied doddering tart shaped self inducing blues

talkin' loneliness' mensch
barenaked
out the window

for brian kim stefans

date
and time
and sign prolly
and in o'haran fashion
have read naught but headlines
since the whiskers of a lynx and since
nike signed tiger nine fine nothing fucking
months, prototype to a giraffe-trap arsenal an
ammo clip kept shelved twixt gestated melatonin & collecteds
yes i'd digest the sugar for you if i could, tread the red and the dead
and the deep blue and i know i'm like an anchor now a pentium one
collicky algorithm yoking your picador processor source of cold sores
and butter on the toolbar the tiger by its tail i know aung san suu kyi is
still in jail all knowing i photographed myself voting buying love minus zero
now in digital but what that denominator "no limit" means by now just be my
guess

slept diaristically
like a pretend pen
the background to history, part 4
woke face down in a book review on blanchot
apparently
"by writing he approaches the unapproachable"
woke
alone, paroled

in which horus rode with hell's entonces
117th a street from morningside to first
hereby blissed out of being in the round
the glass is stained
and i'm behind the tailor
i for hire
have a ploy to ply
cross stitching "best
western" on the pocket of the past
tomorrow's tearsheet winding
white sheet riding
hella burning crosshairs everywhere
staked to capital our
favorite savior storms the nor
the blue and yellow plastic baptist back of worship
like with lightleaks crystallizing lots
misnomer of the enterprise zone
never finished nodding
oh, zone
triple zero crashtest barrier
the steps for nero's dagger's clatter dun been
legislated laid away
library lions tumble off the anti-pedestal plank
a pain in the giraffe,
and in darkness lordly roam the northern s-turn
saltpan prone of harlem
the message in the migrant
bottlenecking thisarraign sacristy ablister
busted natal nightlite paintchip tasty
a needle
and a name for me in duskleak U-G-L-Y

for Ben Davis

what to say when the party turns to boys and girls
coils and connoiters clammed in a
closeted
domestic architectural detail way lee of bass scales
their hands are held in a posey pocket way
arch mouth and soffit frown
targeted as a tomahawk for
pop song pleurisy
this day saying "united states" "united states" "united states"
quote marks look un-mindly on
not gluttonous unison
—repetition is the veterinary part of bloodletter
an old patriot fell down and
tamped out the glowing coals
animals stink and
nasally think
until the else wears out
what is worldly
is the hole in back of the obscura
singing for its sixpence
"lessons from a severed tongue in numberstream"
a dozen unplagued runts atchoo anthem after
tan anathema

bomb

    bomb

        bomb

lo, a
populum
frolics prolix in its
all fall down
whatta lotta
terry malloy
love of
labor's workclothes
my aesthetic
stapled to the chicken
soldered to its black box
audible as
slight
flight data crackle
workers of the world,

----
sign here

name me an empleomane
and I'll find I've got a lot of
right of site to rifle through
another day another
dolor
sipping triggerhappy lampreyade
hallelujah then it's
raining men

this writing is the klan

forced down on all
forms

this was curated
this was canned

a tremendous verse blew in
reminding us the newsprint picture fire
reminded us of banquet camera bowler hat ubiquity
flimsy? fiery? fascisti?
this memo swears the wind blew 'taps'

this fritz; this writing is Sudetentland
writing this
pliny-tinted non event in vicq d'azyr's foramen
friends of the suffix "gate" hocked celine's juvenalia to the late
late variety, "When It's Writ Agog A Star"
I logged an entire proxy

this ironing is bored writing
felled torquey colloquy like a bad noose under glass
who ties anymore? has time to cross and burn?
nails end up penniless
the distant provinces bond
selling telegraphic contact with america, the emperor
via cuckoo pendulums as noose

this this is iffy; that was then
this is
evidence against us

ex of elvin 7 train
korean daily christian stained
with vegetable pilau leakage
a reek of incongruent skullcaps this
saturday of manufacture
in macedonian and tajik even
a business section features
cassowary rearing's
hefty presence over
split-seed planted damsons
if you can't annex, invest
the plenitude comes next
load blanks into the press
under lurid rule of the cure-all allure
überachievers purchase tainted
public education off clark kents
a dominican hid in the wheel well
what's next nascent
next to flushing's fens?
nuisance without finance without romance
a slurred
fluorescent phobia
e pluribus use it or lose it
or come unnerved
a vent in the elevated
fibrillating trenchant
tissue-thin ex-text
and chilly winds don't blow
el diario to bits, it's
cellular, a neverender
calm as those cartels below
firing their phone wires way out of range

"As long an éclairissement as our freckleheaded discount Western discourse can long endure, these here poems could be called rock-n-roll if both roll and rock went on R&R. They are trash compacted; a passionate apologia for the crowd pleaser dashed off with the ubiquity of morse. Learned twenty-third century shit sifters will make no tidy toidy of this poetic bumper crop. Instead its ritual will prove elusive; was this the skinny between barcode beams?"

— *Sister Shibboleth Reinghold, ex-pastor,*
Ecole Normale-Supérieure, tr. C. Eshleman

"I think the teleprompter should be cleaned. Hollowness is popular and satedness is mean. As Maupassant said to his archery set: 'I'm better off for the warts this has caused.' Please read these bellicose peace treaties with well-oiled eyelids; they aren't polarized and their glare is consequently every-spectral. What is pain but the way the monitor bubble reminds us of our corneas? The author's previous books: *Sharp Enough*, *Tearin' Paper*, *Toward a Chordless Bubble Plane*, and *Machiavelli's Kismet* look like lost lenses when compared with this unedited projection. Everything else has been browned out."

—*Araki Yasusada*

"Like real live crispy analog wasps caught by schoolboys in paper cones, the poems of *For the Love of* seem resigned to suffocation. Taking their titles from Creeley's nearly eponymous TV-dinnerless '50's, these poems aren't content to talk like shaky Quakers through the pericardium's plasmic insistence. In fact they're more 'woken, spurred' than spoken word. "I Know a Man" now goes: 'the darkness sus/
                              pects us'
and this book is what we'll goddamned do against it."

—*The Estate of John Rodker*

her monza
and my impreza met
clams at automat
the dumbed down dali
snafu sunset appliqué
stapled to a frappe,
to a lamppost,
licked and then
gummed on
socialism's xerographic notices
it's as plain as the knees in your "place"
ankylosaurs suicide in our
very own seine
the nameless are renamed
large glass windows heft the light in
a crow in every ficus
clichéed trade center atria
throat singers eyed and nosed as entertainment
smoked salmon ate my pinstripes and
stunned this cushion
the lord is a sword swallower in natty pants
the dollar downed again
prominent nominee slakes his constituents' besmeared pioneer
spirit
the dust in the atrium air a
really neat bulimia
a recipe for panoply in all this greenhouse glass
the world's a daze, stained palatial panes
in the penciled in, bracketed, dotted, dashed cadaver
i'm not as lewd as you'd commute
the penitent nepotist with a fart of cold, cold rolaids
a little gingivitis sadness means

prol tax
the institute is nigh, sire
whole overpoets lord their sheer canard over
one more stalag of sentiment in carlsbad: roger rilke,
over.
the lowlands are conefed
traffic in weather found
fronds leafleting Buffalo
hold the anthologies
and the cheese and crust, please
drive an olds to temp jobs in pantheon
troll infested waters with a favorite femur
rock a stone to nope
is this
a delicious baloney?
entendre? not a one
not a hole in none
a five spot on the self to plotz
a congoleum crock
for having has-beens' ISBNs over
and over to tee-hee, see?
the whole spin
in my hand
to kal-el, clark's hair part's the great equator
professor marathon man gulps grecian formula
pounds his nates till the gall falls away
he raised a playing field of even money
dredged the yangtze for an academy to thank
a healthy heft of lofty, penitent coffin scrawl
file under rank

dapper amtrak tieclip
also known as river blindness, my like
has a leak
of knifes,
cyanide,
error and error
another loco motive
a runnedover roll of ectachrome
the trebling of trembling as
segment's rent from tenet
rent from tenant
spent on fretting heretofore asunder
who's to choo-choose who thehell's leg severed meant
this station stop is sol-fa, gamut!
as janet leigh to frank:
I'm one of the original chinese workmen who laid the tracks
ı̣ɯ oυǝ oʇ ʇɥǝ oɹᴉƃᴉuɐʅ ɔɥᴉuǝsǝ ʍoɹʞɯǝu ʍɥo ʅɐᴉ̣q ʇɥǝ ʇɹɐɔʞs
another clowning gory
roans to backhoes ; roads to economic écorché
—conductors still punch holes
democracy, as far as
cargo
crashed in the bracken

designer's dinner
> "last suppers last at
> least as long as it matters"
>
> *—the reader*

a mandarin mechanical cacciatore
let them eat larkspur, sunup
you misspelled *minutus*
how can the salivary gland gain entrée?

how many stylists does it take to screw up an idea?
turn the oven up eleven newtons
the cartesian oilcloth seems
cartesian,
the cleaner the cleanser the lucre the juice

the sweet and low little pink
packeteer keeled over breathless, they say today
about to soufflé his way into the hall of flame
my taste bucks me up, no buts, but
luckily, my cup knuckleth under
i'll have a half a rind, two hives
let the anything-is-beautiful brulé
the thin green line chime
détentes taste al dente today
your asparagus spears twitter
a spoonful of saccharine on this spelling lesson

song of my slough

all
gone
he slew a recreation tube
kept the hermit crabs on the bandsaw
didn't bother holler
off with his pta skimask, in the name of the plotless go-
lightly lollapalooza news

does *viva zapata* mean *living shoes*?
the winner of the race gets to immolate any empty library,
scrape the white off a dozen klines
even nod during mao z.'s big singalong:
"me and my spar-row"
the school play remade *the duelists* starring
god and godard to myriad reviews
and I quote "I quote"
"the one in the sunglasses
seemed to intentionally misread his miscues"
there's the signpost up ahead, it's collicky comme il faut
la vie de chan—ce
anon a
nonagon gone
a chit for constellated blackheads
erasermates as currency
dammit, mirror, limit!

red metaretinals

*"they hoisted her upon the pole as
a signal of distress"*

cut to
will of the people to build canals
anne frank, in fact
browbeat otto for a second telescope
just to have a very large array to train
on sinisterly scuffy mars

a team of surgeons did crack
surgery today
removing all the television news from
horse-healthy movie plots in
readymaded rain

and others in an elevator
strangers,
wince and chuckle at the *goya yoga* joke

hills of beans amount and now I lay me
down to GNP

malawi talkie

africa with flathatted moustaches
crystal stopped, p-p-parfumed houndstooth eau de nickelodeon

frames per p-paternal snicker flicker
private lives in tennis whites i say scuttle
nay, better shuttlecock past *quel* oryx
and for dindin is a carcass carcassone

what a white sauce to have a child by
it's placenta soaked in schistosomiasistic froth
every beggar has a horde to bear
at market, nod and *ya-da-da* for bargains
how i love my little mixture
—soon the bantu jackie cooghan

chaplin on a white shroud from tunis to kwazulu natal
stay spry, wallendas, fill your pith with piss
by way of open air first organ act, hyenas' eyes
half price in fact
a cockle shell, a trinket, six
somali shillings, hell
a ball of lint
makes any two and three or even more reeler
realer
                    REALER!

sitcommie inter
relations
bury my body
canned stepmother and aunt
can and
synapseless cousine half-sib
can't
be seen hunting beachcombers
no how in
regal, legal polynesian season

harelip suture shore
the surf, a sendup of a roux
watch the kingfisher feast on spam
the call of the wild can-it
the snowbubble tomb of
aloha and shalom
now I lei me
sherpa wane will tell me
the lava versus orchid
GNP
sings a poor
Singapore
singalong

just follow the bouncing
landing gear

portal to portal

hawaii is cyan

a light like printing process obsolescence

red and blue ruled newsprint
sold this scribe his
quod scripsi scripsi

without which
a whole deck of
treys stays offset

my supermarket has a calendarian
and three one eyed mendicant managers
and a fever for its
debit flows to blue brochures

on sale in aisle ides
consolidated holidays taste like habeas corpus
a jerky paid a jerky owned
every writ is tied to hiring, every temp a pamphleteer
full moon and new
lobby over fineless print
all type
assumes white light

the ted berrigan cent

plenty money

man and
grant's best friend gone
floating bonds through
thucydidean mania

swell

his dog, FDA, OK's
several slippery forging genes
the nasal helicon has housed since
practically *erectus*

witness huck finn's
whitewashed (I'll say it)
stinky greek
words work the oracle
and course and coreolis down the
mid-chin-and-nosehair trench

god gave us glottises
and irregardless stopped

sleeps with his eyesight,
monoculars and mind trained
leerlessly on
printed matter
john doe number two owned

paranoiac sooth in boots
cyanotyping eyes

sun animalcules in
cornea–window–clock
triangle slave trade

a whole hour
addending hamlet (he says
giving ships of state a wake)

it's house cancer
    –or–
the palaver of reverie
serves his cup of kodak up
if the daily had a
spine to break he'd deign
the cavaliers have clanked the kings
and the mavericks, the magic

the prince finds counting fork tines harrowing

spread the void

induce joking, reader dear
yon concrete cordials pop
dianetic ibid penguins
dummy up the wine god, burning guys
a sip from syphon trachea
bubbling, taking

spin the bottle till it's
stasis' hem you heft
arrest you bless with salivation
your claw marks, bloodsucker
fresh on glacier
a life of finding fondling standardized

today i whet my icepick kaloo kalay
another newsworthy work stoppage
the ball (or is it axe) drops
a nerve net of us pickpockets loves to huddle
a cur rants
at other territory

apply memory like
blue slather for the heartshock
it is medicine and industry and funded
(by some shadow allegiance likely of
the nether and the next)
tastes of emptied phials

fumes from the madeleine plant
of off days ablaze
do tell them from the way
on days dive cauterized

former firecracker snake husk of ways
remember that eminent per diem?

i worked continually
jiggling the toastmaster's scrotum
to jerk the nickel in
knock a little carbon collar sense
between stints
deinstalling memoranda

i made institutes from my weight in paper
Verklate Nacht walkman afternoon commute
true, true, a strand of bent clips is registerial
one day's breath in the ass of the next
two bricks and a 2x6
constitute calico traded and literature sold

get with rectifex, buy apply
lull Caledonia with the same damn
wake up slogan
it was spectral when the poem
emperor or infrastructure
bled non bene libertas venditur

then rain, then receipt
not -eet discrete
watching little shareholder Judy Holliday
drive away in a solid gold candied lack
the audience welled up
that's something happened in a year

caught pilfering the ability to glug
a significant another wrote rondos on united

her "fermented" did deify the yeast
but lots of ubiquities didst mumble me
did did did it?
it's a matter of administer

let's drink to a cyst
wednesday is hump day so more of it
power to it, bloat, overriot, copiousize
pin editorialissimus to a chloroform board
we're breathing
is enlightenment this weekend?

i renally need a love letter
bely a tribal sweetie gets her commits on his
pony expression
but luck being nothing to manx at means even
mail carriers wish for ripping innards
the chrysalises for dinner at cafe heavenesque

every serve a let in every port
the government will ban elastic
but children everywhere
run rustic for replacement tracheas
and more frantic as the music
plea bargains noticability

one mother's everyday i book write
saw in sonar a militia
sandbagged in his bladder
the guillotine fell back across the 18th century
though wyatt berry stapp earp
lived to see the stock market crash and penicillin

0-fer i remember can i say can i
see by the by lines
diapering light
when it rains
there's something tabloid to hide under
but by then it's then again

stunted stewed haploid haole
yelling at the mirror is the prison system
leased to the justice department on veteran's day
a means of stamping the anomaly with
scheherazade's pass key and
faking making

lost year i cost
this many whimpers
sticking his strike counter out of camera wrangle
the walk to tic tac toe a
pound sign beleaguerdly begetting
yanqui stay

the glass half filibustered
rustler of nullitive necked
charmless & noble inhibitors
and even proteus got a window box
figure office walls and pole stars
your head in there somewhere

Tim Davis was born in Malawi, a month before the moon shot. Early influences include Reggie Jackson, Eugene Ionesco, Jif Peanut Butter, and Jimmy Carter's hair. An heir to the Hammerhead Shark Milk fortune, he was educated in Photography at Bard College, in Poetry at The Ear Inn, & in Photography again at Yale. During a tour of duty as an editor at New Directions, he produced two chapbooks of poetry, *The Analogy Guild* (Arras Press), and *My Life in Politics –or– A History of N=A=R=R=A=T=I=V=E Film* (Object Editions/Poetscoop), and a monograph on the campiness of pandas. Late influences include Ukelele Ike, Emily D., Buster Keaton, and capital expansion. He is increasingly certain that art is all about errands, and has said about his writing, "quod scripsi scripsi."

Eight hundred copies
of *Dailies* printed November 1999
at McNaughton & Gunn, Saline, Michigan,
of which 15 are numbered in Roman
numerals I – XV, & signed
by the poet.